BIRD IN A WILDERNESS

Published by Telltale Press
49 Silverdale Road
Eastbourne BN20 7AY
© Telltale Press 2023

Edited by Brian Docherty, Stephanie Gaunt, Robin Houghton & Antony Mair
Cover image Judith Shaw

A CIP catalogue record for this book is available from the British Library

ISBN 978-0-9928555-8-1

Bird in a Wilderness

A Hastings Stanza Anthology

"The poet grapples with his own shadow
The poet cries like a bird in a wilderness."

Zbigniew Herbert – *On Troy*

Supporting The Refugee Buddy Project

A percentage of the profits from the sale of this anthology will go to The Refugee Buddy Project.

Now a registered charity, The Refugee Buddy Project is a refugee- and migrant-led organisation that stands in solidarity with people seeking refuge in Hastings, Rother and Wealden. It works to create a culture of welcome where people seeking refuge can thrive. It does this by offering advice, advocacy and psychosocial support and connecting people seeking refuge with volunteer buddies from the community.

The charity was founded by Rossana Leal who came to the UK in the 1970s with her family, escaping the Pinochet regime in Chile. They were taken in by the mining community in Scotland, and received a welcome which stayed with Rossana for the rest of her life. In 2017 she felt compelled to recreate that welcome in Hastings, and so she set up The Refugee Buddy Project.

For more information and other ways you can donate, please visit the website at **therefugeebuddyproject.org**

Contents

Foreword

Stanza groups are the result of an initiative by The Poetry Society, the UK's national advocacy organisation for poetry. They comprise poetry lovers, throughout the UK and abroad, who engage in a variety of activities, from workshops to competitions and festivals. Each Stanza has a nominated Representative who is the official link to The Poetry Society.

I founded the Hastings Stanza, and became its Representative, in 2014. I had been dubious about numbers, but found an unexpected resource in Hastings Writers Group, where some were keen to focus more closely on poetry.

The core activity of Hastings Stanza has always been monthly workshopping, when each person brings a poem for feedback. The number of people attending varies between six and twelve, and the emphasis is on positive criticism. It has been a source of both pride and joy for me to have watched the quality of writing improve beyond recognition since we first met. A number of members have published collections and/or won competitions. Most have had poems published in poetry magazines. Equally, however, there are those who write for the pleasure of it, without a wish for publication.

This anthology is of poems by some of those regularly attending meetings. The section containing biographical details of the poets concerned also gives indications of how some poems have changed following discussion in Stanza meetings.

I hope you enjoy the results.

Antony Mair

Hillman Imp

I gave him a lift
in the ex-police car, water
dripping down my neck
from the hole in the roof
where the blue light used to be.

He was in the International
Marxist Group. We had
vigorous discussions
about the Revolution, how
Women Hold up Half the Sky.

One night staying drunk
at a tutor's house
I hauled his clothes off
and pulled him into me.
The last time we spoke

the radiator boiled over.
I sold the car for fifty quid
to someone who thought
he could fix it, but I knew better.
The cylinder head was cracked.

Judith Shaw

The Cordwainer's Son

They were his familiars:
fine hides from Cordoba, contoured with their faint
lifelines, shaped on the last, the waxy top-skin
pliant in his hands. So he'd started with the boots,
unhooking the buttons with studied attention,
a row of silvered moons. Only then

daring to look up:
she'd sat on the bench amongst the marking
wheels and size sticks, put him in mind
of a sleek-winged goose rafting the skies,
with her cambric dress and the skein of her hair,
the blue-black stockings

cupped in his palms.
Now he works a shoe with the stretching pliers,
punches holes with a sharpened awl.
His eyes are clouded, the sole knife slips,
a hand knocks over the tin of nails; they roll
to the edge and fall like rain.

Jill Fricker

She Blames it on the Heat

Spilt sugar. A dropped spoon.
Arrival of an ant column
scaling the table leg.
These are tricks of the heat.

Her comforts come in waves.
A little dog's self-soothing breath,
a girl's blue bead necklace. A breeze,
or the step-sister of a breeze.

Houseleek flesh is a solace,
fattened to the edge of green.
Her gaze paddles in the shadows
between the leaves

but when she looks beyond,
smoke parasols the macchia,
set on fire in the distant hills
that lap and lap the sea.

Evening thunder growls, no rain
to douse it. Too few tourists,
war reports on the radio; all, all,
she blames it on the heat.

Alex Josephy

The Last of the Romanovs

Friday night at the country club
the last of the Romanovs
mumbled into her consommé
while her husband parcelled leftover salmon
to feed Toby, Kitty, Otto
Coco, Mitzi, and Pearl
the last of her loyal subjects.

In the car park afterwards, she beat him with her fists
screaming Russian curses.
Not Russian, an old general muttered.
Polack. Definitely Polack.

No one ever knew how they survived,
feasting on rumours and promises.
Well, wouldn't you go a little bit crazy
if those damn commies killed your family?

Yesterday the police took her to the county institution,
her husband crying and begging
for his princess. As the door swung open
the cats left one by one,
heading through the weeds and rusting cans
proud tails curled like question marks.

Andrea Samuelson

Note: During her long life, Anna Anderson was believed by many to be the missing Grand Duchess Anastasia. A DNA test long after her death proved she was a Polish factory worker named Franziska Schanzkowska.

Away for the Duration
after Duncan Grant's 'Four Seasons' in Berwick Church, 1944

How can she concentrate on the sermon
in this distracting nave? She sees her Timothy
in the painted roundels, each season of longing
cruelly inscribed on the rood screen:

the hand that bends the horse and plough
into a long furrow; the horse's crescent ears,
its jaunty raised fetlock; the turning wheel,
everything coming right.

He's in the harvest scene, where reapers hug
sheaves, re-enact that awkward spark
– their first dance, bodies still separate at the hip,
eyes squeezed tight against hope.

How can she kneel on an embroidered stool
while Tim stands or falls without her knowing?
A river curves across two panels; one is flushed
pink, the other dark as dance-hall kisses.

She holds him in a basket of apples
freshly pulled from the tree; oil paint apples,
but they smell of Eve, smell of snapped twig,
bruise against her palm.

If he has fallen, she'll take him on her shoulder
like that woman with the firewood bundle,
at first as light as kindling, later heavier
than she thinks she can bear.

Alex Josephy

Artemisia Gentileschi: Self-Portrait

Yes, I am Artemisia, even my name
is Artistic, art is woven into my very
being, but I am also named after

Artemis, and I am well versed
in her mysteries, which since you
are a mere man, I cannot share

with you, but know this, Sir,
if you commission me, I shall
give you my best work, I never

short-change my patrons, but if
you want realism, I say *What
is that?* Look at me, I am a real

woman, a real working artist,
I am my own inspiration, look
at my hands, look into my eyes,

I am so much more than you
can imagine, I can paint things
men can not, but my studio

is private, no-one but me holds
the key, and know this, I have no
assistants or pupils, what I will

deliver to you shall be all my own,
and I am never late or absent,
I do not have the luxury of being

like Caravaggio or Michelangelo,
I am first among equals, so let us
agree my price and shake on it.

Brian Docherty

14

Not Preying

In the genial warmth of the evening,
in a side street off the market where,
after shopping, people wander in search
of *tapas* and *cerveza* or a glass of *Rioja*,
he kneels under a streetlamp, lays out his chalks,
marks a rectangle on the pavement three feet by two.

He outlines something,
fills the background with muted greens,
uses his fingertips to smudge and
blur the edges.

A crowd gathers.

He chooses a vivid green to draw a body,
blends red for shadows,
yellow on the abdomen, white for highlights.
Four back limbs emerge, thin, angled.
A triangular head with bulging eyes
turns ninety degrees to scrutinise the audience.
Long antennae wave. Spiked forelegs fold
in a characteristic posture of prayer,
but look more pugilistic than devotional.

A round of applause.
Coins rattle his box.
He's earned his supper.

Sandra Andrews

A Cartoon Return

Side by side we watched cartoons
like cartoons of kids watching cartoons,
bending, twisting our small bodies, both

holding our breath, flattening ourselves,
trying to slip between floorboards to reach
the Saturday den of a mouse superhero.

We bent and twisted all our storylines
to tall tales, outwitting the cat fiend,
taking leaps unfeasible, daring

to eat impossible cakes with bombs in,
lighting each other's fuses and plotting
to blow the place to smithereens.

We planned our teen getaways, invisible
in Chromacolor stealth-cloaked
ACME motorbike and sidecar.

This Saturday, forty years on, we return.
I will take an oversized frying pan,
swing it with animated precision

as you engineer distracting explosions
and we blunder, side by side once more,
into the same old trip-wires, fall

into pits of snakes, time-out the axes
dangling, the rows of shiny spikes
meant to pin us to ourselves.

Oenone Thomas

Speech

Flings. I've had a few. But then again that was in the sexed-up nineties. We thought the world was going to end, computer bugs blast planes from the sky – so why not. Every meeting or awayday shot adrenaline through our veins. We fell into each other with the speed and shock of a zip-wire. And who are we talking about here? Fiancés. Bosses. Co-workers. Lads on the up. Dads. Me. There were two good men. One I googled years later and saw his grizzled old chops grinning from Darlington to Crewe. Out of the race and coaching kids for kicks. The other cashed in his chips and tried farming but the drugs don't work and never have no matter how you pray. Flings are the edge-pieces of the jigsaw: satisfying at the time but still a big blank centre yawns back at you and the picture is only complete when the last sodding bit of sky or sea or cud-chewing beast snaps into place. We thought the world was going to end on the millionth click so we courted chaos, dived head-first into some kind of love till our brains burst and the meeting room lights went out. Anyway. Ladies and gentlemen, charge your glasses. To the bride and groom.

Robin Houghton

Rosemary

The night my father touched me, something died.
He showed me I had power I could use.
Some doors are best left closed – don't look inside.

There's none believe me now. They say I've lied,
that I'm a monster wanting headline news.
The night my father touched me, something died.

My husband freed me and became my guide.
I learnt to find excitement in a bruise.
Some doors are best left closed – don't look inside.

I felt my power when the children cried
but kept my calm – Fred had the shorter fuse.
The night my father touched me, something died.

I had my pleasure-room, where I could hide
my masks and gags, my dildos, whips and screws.
Some doors are best left closed – don't look inside.

The body parts were proof that I denied.
The judge said I was always free to choose,
but when my father touched me, something died.
Some doors are best left closed – don't look inside.

Antony Mair

play time

the girls' playground sloped at such a degree
fear trickled from the underarms of rivals
over from Middle Park to beat us at netball

when not handstanding against the wall
during break we linked arms and stomped uphill
chanting *who wants to play* then downhill *join*

on the end until ten or more of us teamed up
in a streamer   a wave of laughter   the last ones
swung around and running then uphill again

and always the Alpha girls would decide who
will be babies who the eagles those who swoop
and kidnap babies while babies would cower

or creep free to imagine themselves rescued
or eaten up there by the outside toilets under
a corrugated roof the secret eyrie was a nest

of babies crouched in a whisper out of sight
of the netball court quietly terrified of games
or dinnertime waiting to be let in at the bell

Robin Houghton

Catching Covid

This is how it creeps up closer…
An invisible arrival from a stranger.

It's like a winter harbour in the north.
Fogged. Unfocussed. Cold and dark.

A scratchiness inside the throat.
Had she swallowed barbs or nettles?

She looked through her long list of symptoms:
irritations from ageing; her reactions to dust.

She slammed the door against the spiders.
That room held webs. It smelled of corpses.

She imagined she had been sedated.
It felt like lying underwater, to dream upon

the edge of nothing.

Annie Maclean

Empty Nest

On days of boredom
(there were so many)
we would spread out a roll of wallpaper
on the threadbare carpet
and I would lay you down to draw your shape

like the outline of a crime scene.
Look, you can see yourself.
You coloured in eyes, mouth, nose,
gave yourself hair made out of wool,
and clothing out of pretty scraps.

Though I loved you like no other
I was jealous of my life, always finding ways
to get away.
Look at me, Mum. Watch me.
Long time, long time, long time.

Your shadow grew from year to year.
Now, the empty doorways stare.
I clean out your room, think how to make use
of what is spare, and I trace
your missing outline in the air.

Andrea Samuelson

Darkroom

Remember how it used to be.

You'd load a camera. Take pictures.
Rush to the darkroom. Feel
into the lightproof womb,
slide the film into the developer,
stop solution, wash, hang to dry
till it was ready for the light.
Those tiny squares of images
black as white, white as black.

You never printed them.

I spent thirty years in the dark
trying to understand
until the scar of your back
faded into the dense evening.

Judith Shaw

The Nightmare

Below an empty tin sky the horizon folded in sea fret
grey overlapping grey, not one gull breaks the absolute silence

and in the mist a child's starfish body floats wrapped
in red wool, tendrils of hair curl through the waves

I scream into the stubborn unbreakable silence, wade in waist deep
to cradle dead limbs, each step forces me into deeper water

still she floats beyond my reach, red rivulets run from her body
become carbon copy children bobbing in a blood red sea

I return night after night never knowing who to save first

Catherine Sweeney

Wave

The cold weight of it hitting
my shoulders.
I sagged.
It went down inside my coat.
I could feel it swilling around the brim of my hat
swirling at my ankles.
My sodden trousers were falling down
my shoes full.
It took a moment
to understand a whole wave
had come up
and over
the wide harbour arm.
That I was on a slight incline
slipping sideways in inches of backwash
towards the edge.
I pulled one foot clear of the flow
placed it higher up the promenade
then the other until
step by step
on ridged soles
I reached the arches
and a passage
to safety
a waterfall of sea
at my side.

Sandra Andrews

Sonnet of Sadness

She crossed the Harbour Field alone:
she chose to use the time to think
on The Many Things She Had To Ponder.
She carried a bag she'd packed,
bulging with her Current Worries:
a heaviness.
A stickiness.
The irritations from that wretched virus
plus the sadness and the shame of Brexit.
She raised her hand to touch the air
to feel the boiling of the rain.
Dust hissed. Time passed.
She remembered what she had forgotten –
things lost inside the climate's change...

Annie Maclean

Silent Praise

Praise the Lord, praise the weather,
praise your mother, praise yourself

if you have done something worthwhile
or maybe if you have just done nothing

and not made the world a worse place
today, but if you find nothing or no-one

praiseworthy, then maybe it's time
for meditation, or chant a mantra.

If you ever visit a Zen temple
with a silent table in the dining hall,

make the right gesture, and if invited,
sit and enjoy your lunch in silence,

then go into the kitchen and take part
in the silent washing up meditation

for which you will not be praised,
because that work is there to be done

with a willing hand, and mindfulness
is a perfect form of praise, as long as

you don't expect to accumulate merit
towards your next incarnation.

Brian Docherty

Pearl

I dreamed I was back among the black rocks,
alone with the dead crows and a fear of falling,

woke to sudden rain, and someone calling
your name. My brittle shell has developed cracks

where an old darkness leaks out, and there is sand
in the soft tissue of my complacency.

I hear a door close, trust that you can see
how a dark path is lit up by the laughter of friends.

There was a wind last night, after the rain,
and then stillness, waiting for your return.

Robin Renwick

Meandering down to Hastings Old Town

Someone's left a Venetian blind outside their gate,
  brand new, still sealed in its plastic wrapper.
    Leave it, keep on walking.
        ...A vaporetto grumbles on its way
          from Rialto to San Marco, passing
            the blind Venetian, tap-tapping along the riva,
        white stick probing green-slimed cobbles.
      Below, dark water sucks and smacks its lips...
Too near the edge, perhaps?
      No, not this time.
        ...He's shuffling round a corner,
          down a shaded calle by the broken fountain,
        towards a smell of frying garlic.
     His favourite ristorante...
Leave it, live in the moment as
  road drops down to steel grey sea,
    distant ships like black crayon smudges,
      a grey whale hummock, Beachy Head.
        That glinting window across the bay
         might mean sun in Eastbourne.
           ... In his usual corner seat,
          the blind Venetian sniffs his wine,
       crumbles bread between his fingers,
    eager for osso bucco, or saltimbocca, fagioli....
Or what's that Venetian dish... *risi e bisi?*
    Rice and peas.
      Not like Jamaican rice and peas,
        those peas are really beans...
Now, what did I want from town?

Stephanie Gaunt

28

Monastery Lane

It's summer. With the sun on our faces
we walk towards the corner plot,

kneel to push our hands into dark
friable soil, pull the weeds

to clear a path to my grandparents.
As my father digs the flower bed

his words transform the air,
weaving images to sow the past

into my present. I feel the comforting
weight of my grandma's hand, the lilting

humour of my grandfather's wit.
I brush the soil from my skirt,

knees stained grass green,
notes of the Latin Mass spiced with incense

and the scent of decaying roses tumble
into Monastery Lane.

                        Holding tight
to my father's hand, we say goodbye,

close the gate.

Catherine Sweeney

Watching the River Dwyfor

The chest of the water rises
on boulders which inflate
as the river flexes
speaks to its bank
whispers to the quiet fern
and the holly shouts back
with tales of what has filtered downstream
from the rain garden, past vigorous roots
to the melancholy power of shade.

What the river says as it
brushes by the trees that bend into a figure of 6
strikes the flowers dumb.

The grass lies down by its closed mouth
shuffles blades
silenced by a flick of wild water
its current, winding through rivulets
tricks me into singing
bashful, only the river listening.

Jackie Hutchinson

West Cork Morning

It's as if I've lost all hearing:
at this hour the silence throbs.
Beyond the double-glazed French windows
blue-tits hop from shrub to shrub
and the meadow falls to an inlet
stretching its grey mirror
across to the boatyard masts.
In the distance a miniature figure
walks along the empty road,
disappears up a drive.

Even if I were outside
the silence, interrupted by bird chatter,
would fold its gentleness around my ears.
No wind today. The pieris holds out
flamed fans of yellow and orange,
motionless.

On the other side of the bay
a ruined tower holds a past
of shouts and bloodshed,
now long gone. Here wild garlic
throngs the roadside, and the ferns
unfurl young fronds
with fearful tenderness.

Antony Mair

Mountain

Stone,
and cold.
A loose path –
and we walk on
out of a grey mist
to where the crag rises.
A high ridge – a hard scramble
in a thin, cold light. We follow
uncertain tracks, we move through the day's
changes of weather – blue skies, sudden squalls –
deserted places lost in mist and rainbows.

We have lived our lives close to the edge – seeking those

deserted places. Lost in mist and rainbows,
changes of weather, blue skies, sudden squalls,
uncertain tracks – we move through the days
in a thin, cold light. We follow
a high ridge, a hard scramble
to where the crag rises
out of a grey mist –
and we walk on
a loose path
and cold
stone.

Robin Renwick

Stork's Flight / *Nid de Cigogne*

We subside on loungers,
sip peppermint tea, watch the sky
because once we saw the stork
fly overhead to her nest.
Not so rare here:
a nightly flight,
but so easy to miss.

On the riad's roof in Marrakesh:
breaths of jasmine,
kaleidoscope lights,
muted Medina music.
Indigo floods corners,
where bamboo whispers in clay urns.

There she is, we say,
hold our breath, smile.
Watch steady, downward beat of wings,
outstretched neck,
deliberate flight
through polished stars.

Storks bring; storks take.
We hold hands tight against the taking,
pray for the soft fall
and kiss
of white feathers.

Roz Balp

Winter Wheel

It's so cold in the garden
and the wind is relentless
it soars through the air like a hurricane
ripping the old olives from the trees.
Our cat sleeps warily on the olived floor
the sun, a vision
so low
it is blocked out by the stuffed houses
but each day the sun rises a little higher
lengthening its rays
and soon
it will be spring.

Jackie Hutchinson

Kuniyoshi (Tanka)

Bellflower blue still blooms,
crimson sun-leached to plum's blush:
a Kuniyoshi.

Children smile and play
in loose, patterned kimono.
I see them running:
flat white faces, bright black eyes;
hear laughter, rub of cotton.

The pressed-ink image,
with cherry block etched, stilled on
mulberry paper.

Roz Balp

The High Line

You wouldn't think to place it here,
floating, running on abandoned rails,
dressed in lavenders and cotton-ball
creams, duck-egg blues.
And yet this is perfect, a sky-hung park;
a boardwalk spanning the twenty blocks
from West 34th to Gansevoort.
New York strolls above itself
to stare at grey-green grasses mirrored
in glass, three-flowered maples and bottlebrush
buckeyes high-fiving their towering reflections.
Mockingbirds mimic the car alarms
and mourning doves in the Chinese fringe trees
are strung like lanterns; their muted sobs
raise the meatpacker ghosts
to glimpse the Hudson
through derelict lots,
flowing south.

Jill Fricker

Almuñécar Municipal Market – Notice of Demolition

I can hear the bell belonging
to Iglesia El Salvador ringing
for market hall porters
uncoiling shuddering hoses.
Shutters clatter half-closure.

At the entrance two rabbits hang,
one hook between them, reduced
by noon sun, even their shadows
gone. Week on week they seem
foreign as foreign.

I'm late, I pass fish afloat
in ice melt, net a kilo of scales,
shells, handful of bones tossed,
a cheap curse in wax paper.
Deal sealed.

Almonds raised in sacks
rattle their little armour. Olives,
further from their nature,
huddle in vats. Twists of herbs,
for every pain, are drying.

Saffron. Lemon oil for dressing hair.
Old sherry vinegar. Sliced hearts
of lettuce, their stems milky,
alert a thirst for rootedness.
Exit – the bell stills.

Sluice water and brushing
prepares the ground. Sounds beyond
of waves fizzing.
The street empties –
refills with heat.

Oenone Thomas

Visit to the Tito Bustillo cave

A painted horse leaps towards us, wide-eyed, mouth agape,
as our guide sweeps torchlight round the cavern.
Red ochre reindeer, bison, more horses shaded mauve,
spines curved against the strata.

Rapid Spanish echoes off the walls, over our English heads.
A deluge of words, too fast for us to follow.
Looking down, shuffling our feet on the muddy floor,
we understand nothing.

A man translates. 'People painted that same patch of rock,
over and over, for ten thousand years. We don't know why.
Perhaps this place was sacred.' I ask a question,
he doesn't hear me.

The torch flickers across grids of cross-hatched lines,
scored into the rock. We stare, searching for meaning.
The group moves on, light recedes to a pinprick, vanishes.
We're all in the dark.

Stephanie Gaunt

Note: The earliest paleolithic paintings in the cave in Northern Spain
are at least 25,000 years old.

Biographical Notes and Comments

Sandra Andrews went to art college in the swinging sixties and taught art and practised painting before taking up writing after retiring. Her work remains strongly connected to observable reality.

On 'Not Preying': 'When this poem was shown to the Stanza Group it had six stanzas, what is now the fourth stanza having a break between line three and four. The final stanza, now three sentences on separate lines, was originally written as one sentence in a single line.'

Roz Balp taught English for 35 years and now strives to shape the language into poems. She finds the discipline and the creative process therapeutic.

On 'Kuniyoshi': 'This poem was workshopped at Stanza in its original form of seven haiku, and several members pointed out that the final part was too abstract to be a true haiku. When I reshaped it into a tanka, I discarded those lines, and focused instead on concrete images. This sharper version won the National Association of Writers & Groups competition.'

Brian Docherty was born in Glasgow and lived in North London for forty years before moving to St Leonards-on-Sea. He has published eight books, most recently *The View From The Villa Delirium* (2021).

On 'Artemisia Gentileschi: Self-portrait': 'This poem was written in a session of Words for Wellbeing Writers Group in 2020 on the theme of "identity". It was critiqued at Hastings Stanza, and revised accordingly afterwards.'

Jill Fricker has had her poetry placed in competitions including Poets Meet Politics, Bare Hands International, and Sentinel Literary Quarterly, and published in poetry anthologies and the *Morning Star.*

On 'The Cordwainer's Son': 'When workshopped, it was suggested I take out some of the adjectives and trust that the young shoemaker's emotions would still be apparent. The group really liked the inclusion of the nineteenth-century shoemaker's tools, so in the final stanza I reworked the poem slightly with the tools providing the metaphors for the young man's feeling of loss.'

Stephanie Gaunt started writing poems following retirement. She has been presented with a cup by the late Queen for winning a national poetry competition, and has published a collection of her poems.

On 'Visit to the Tito Bustillo cave': 'This was written after a visit to Spain in 2019. The Stanza group helped me to understand and avoid one of the most common pitfalls for the newer writer – too much "telling" rather than "showing". I had also introduced a humorous element, which the group felt was not congruent with the theme of the poem. I cut this, making the poem much stronger.'

Robin Houghton is widely published. Her fourth pamphlet *Why? And Other Questions* (2019) won the Live Canon Pamphlet Competition. She co-hosts the podcast *Planet Poetry.*

On 'play time': 'At Stanza, it was pointed out that "eagles" was repeated in the middle of the fourth stanza, so I changed it from "eagles got to swoop" to "those who swoop"' It was commented that there was a sense of strangeness to the story, so I tried to further disorient the reader by giving it a new title, which I think feels more menacing than the previous "Babies & Eagles".'

Jackie Hutchinson is a member of both Brighton and Hastings Stanza groups, and a regular reader at her local Eastbourne Poetry Cafe. Her work was commended in *Magma*'s 2021/22 competition.

On 'Watching the River Dwyfor': 'First workshopped at Hastings Stanza in June 2020, the poem has changed radically. It is a much tighter, less rambling poem which has benefited from a loss of personal narrative and over-reflection. Apart from the odd residential workshop, I had never submitted my poetry to regular discussion. Stanza has improved my editing process immensely.'

Alex Josephy lives in Rye, East Sussex, and sometimes in Italy. Recent publications include *Again Behold the Stars*, Cinnamon Press, 2023, and *Naked Since Faversham*, Pindrop Press, 2020.

On 'Away for the Duration': 'I changed various lines after thinking about the comments made at Stanza. I gave the absent soldier/ sweetheart a name, to make it clearer throughout who "he" is. I changed "pretty Berwick church" at the opening (too pretty!) to "this distracting nave." And the title "The Duration" became "Away for the Duration", with a note of the date of the painting too, to make the WW2 context more explicit.'

Annie Maclean is Scottish. Her *The Garden/er* was published by Hedgehog Press in 2019. She enjoys exploring form. She has recently experienced heart problems and sees this as a response to the climate emergency.

On 'Sonnet of Sadness': 'After workshopping with the group, I removed some lines that were confusing people and deleted a final conclusion that did not seem to be adding anything. I ended up with fourteen lines, so worked it into a sonnet. There is a deliberate *volta* around Brexit, and a reminder of climate emergency at the end.'

Antony Mair has published three collections, most recently *A Suitcase Filled with Hope* (Live Canon, 2021). He was awarded first prize in the 2022 Live Canon International Poetry Competition.

On 'West Cork Morning': 'I revised this poem in a couple of places following a Stanza meeting. The line referring to "bird chatter" had "punctuated" rather than the present "interrupted", and was thought ponderous. And the reference to the miniature figure was shortened from the original version.'

Robin Renwick is a retired textile designer who grew up in Sussex and now lives in Hastings. His poems have been published in *Agenda, Sarasvati* and *Dream Catcher.*

On 'Mountain': 'This mirror poem started out as a diamond shape entitled "Hill Walk". After workshopping it in a Stanza meeting I separated the two halves and changed the title, unifying the image, title and content, and greatly strengthening the poem.'

Born in America, **Andrea Samuelson** has lived most of her life in Hastings. Her short fiction and poetry has been published in many magazines and her poetry collection *Cradle Song* (based on her great-grandmother's incarceration in an asylum) was published in 2011.

On 'Empty Nest': 'The poem lost most of its final stanza due to the group's comments, and definitely for the better. It's easy when you're writing a first or even second or third draft, to explain too much.'

Judith Shaw completed the Poetry School MA in 2023. She was shortlisted in the 2022 AONB Best Landscape Poem; her work is in *Ten Poems about Getting Older* (Candlestick Press).

On 'Darkroom': 'I brought this poem to Stanza and was asked useful questions which clarified my intentions in the poem as well as giving me useful suggestions about how to sharpen the language.'

Catherine Sweeney joined Hastings Stanza in 2020 and is a member of the Poetry Society with poems published in *Between the Lines 2021,* produced by CityLit, and *The Galway Review.*

On 'Monastery Lane': 'In a Stanza workshop I was encouraged to experiment with the form of this poem and helpful suggestions were made to tighten the narrative.'

Oenone Thomas was brought up in South Wales and southern Spain. She is a writer and chocolatemaker. Her poems are increasingly appearing in magazines and she is working towards an MA at the Poetry School, London.

On 'A Cartoon Return': 'The group helped me with the poem's coherence. It was especially helpful to hear the consensus that my original choice of last line – "meant to startle apparitions" – needed to be stronger and fit the sense of the poem better. I later changed this to "meant to pin us to ourselves".'

Acknowledgements

'Kuniyoshi' (Roz Balp) won the National Association of Writers & Groups Competition.

'The Cordwainer's Son' (Jill Fricker) was placed second in the Four Counties Open Competition.

'The Highline' (Jill Fricker) was shortlisted in the Writing the City poetry competition (2015), and was published in the Writing The City anthology.

'Speech' (Robin Houghton) was published in *Prole* 33.

'She Blames it on the Heat' (Alex Josephy) was published in *morphrog* 26 in January 2023.

'Mountain' (Robin Renwick) was published in *Dream Catcher* 43.

'Pearl' (Robin Renwick) was published in *Agenda* 'Scentings' issue, Vol 28 numbers 1-2.

'Monastery Lane' (Catherine Sweeney) was published in *The Galway Review* in September 2022.

'Almuñécar Municipal Market – Notice of Demolition' (Oenone Thomas) was published in *Magma* 86.

Cover artist **Judith Shaw** lives and works in St Leonards on Sea. She explores different materials in her artworks including painting and printmaking, often using non-traditional methods to create semi-abstract and evocative pieces. For her, making work is a process of exploring the potential of materials, as well as being sensitive to what the piece itself needs.

Contact: 07909 62564 or judith@judithshaw.info